D1014532

Gardening For Kids

A Kid's Guide to Container Gardening

Stephanie Bearce

Mitchell Lane
PUBLISHERS

P.O. Box 196
Hockessin, Delaware 19707
Visit us on the web: www.mitchelllane.com
Comments? email us: mitchelllane@mitchelllane.com

Gardening For Kids

A Backyard Flower Garden for Kids
A Backyard Vegetable Garden for Kids
Design Your Own Butterfly Garden
Design Your Own Pond and Water Garden
A Kid's Guide to Container Gardening
A Kid's Guide to Landscape Design
A Kid's Guide to Making a Terrarium
A Kid's Guide to Organic Gardening
A Kid's Guide to Perennial Gardens

ABOUT THE AUTHOR: Stephanie Bearce has been making container gardens since she was five years old. In kindergarten she planted lima bean seeds in a pot. She writes: "I was very proud of having my own plant. I loved gardens and plants so much that in college I took classes in plant science." Stephanie worked as the director of children's education at the Missouri Botanical Garden, where she taught children how to grow plants and how to take care of them. As a science teacher, she has helped many students build container gardens, butterfly gardens, and native plant gardens. She lives in Missouri.

Printing 1 2 3 4 5 6 7 8 9

PUBLISHER'S NOTE: The facts on which the story in this book is based have been thoroughly researched. Documentation of such research can be found on page 46. While every possible effort has been made to ensure accuracy, the publisher will not assume liability for damages caused by inaccuracies in the data, and makes no warranty on the accuracy of the information contained herein.

Library of Congress Cataloging-in-Publication Data
Bearce, Stephanie.
A kid's guide to container gardening / by Stephanie Bearce.
p. cm. — (A Robbie reader. Gardening for kids)
Includes bibliographical references and index.
ISBN 978-1-58415-814-1 (library bound)
1. Container gardening—Juvenile literature. I. Title. II. Series: Robbie reader. Gardening for kids.
SB418.B39 2009
635.9'86—dc22

2009001314

PLB

Contents

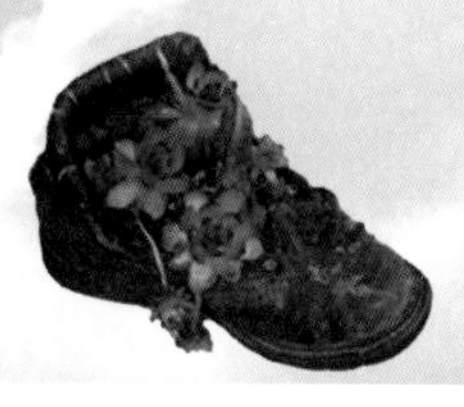

Words in **bold** type can be found in the glossary.

Introduction

Container gardening is gooey, messy, and lots of fun—just like planting a garden in the ground. What's great about container gardening, though, is that you can move your plants all around your yard, arrange them on a patio, hang them from a ceiling, or use them to brighten the inside of your house.

Container gardens can be large or small, with many kinds of plants or just one. They can be in any sort of container, too—a plain flowerpot or one you've painted yourself, a pair of old boots, or even a decorated coffee can.

Before you begin your container garden, you must get permission from your family. They can help

you find a place that will be safe for the plants. They will also show you where it is okay to make a mess. A good gardener cleans up after every project.

When you are choosing plants, if you want to put your container outside, you will need to know about **hardiness** (HAR-dee-ness) **zones**. These areas of the United States have the same types of climate. Find your zone on a USDA Hardiness Zone Map (http://www.growit.com/zones/). Then check out the seed packet or label that comes with your plant to be sure it will survive in your zone.

It is exciting to help plants grow from tiny **seedlings** into big beautiful flowers. It's fun to dig in the dirt and water the plants. When you build a container garden, there's always something new and messy to do.

Chapter 1

Getting Started

Do you like digging in the dirt, messing in the mud, and playing with plants? If so, container gardening could be a great hobby for you. It is a wonderful way to learn how to garden without using lots of land.

Container gardens are small groups of plants that are grown in pots, tubs, or wooden boxes. Container gardens don't take up much space. This makes them perfect for people who don't have yards or who live in apartments.

Container gardens are **portable**. You can move the pots from one spot to another without hurting the plants. These gardens are easy to grow because they don't require large amounts of water. They will grow anywhere there is sunlight.

People have been making container gardens for thousands of years. **Archaeologists** (ar-kee-AH-loh-jists) have found evidence of container gardens in Egyptian and Roman ruins. The Romans grew flowers and plants in pots on their patios. Later in history, monks grew plants in containers and used the plants to make medicines.

If you want to build a container garden, your first job is to find a good location. Look for a sunny spot on a patio or by a window. Sometimes

taking care of your garden can get messy, so this should be a place where spilling water or **soil** will not damage your home.

Porches and balconies look beautiful when they are filled with container gardens. They make great gardening spaces for people who don't have yards.

Look for a place that gets lots of sunshine. Most plants like four to six hours of sunlight a day. You will need to count the hours of sunlight. Use a clock to figure out how much sunshine is in your garden spot. Watch in the morning for the sun to shine on your chosen spot. Write down the time. Watch

Plants for Containers and the Amount of Sunshine They Need to Grow

Full Sun	Partial Shade	Full Shade
Croton	Violas	Chinese Evergreen
Pansies	Dracaena	Peace Lily
Cyclamen	Begonia	Sansevieria
Hibiscus	Watermelon Peperomia	Coleus

throughout the day to see when the sunlight moves away from the spot. Write down that time. Look at the two times you have written, and then count the number of hours between them. If there are four to six hours of sunshine, it is a good place for a garden of sun-loving plants.

	What time sunlight hits	What time sunlight leaves	Total hours of sunlight	Number of hours plant needs
Morning				
Afternoon				
Evening				

The amount of sunshine is important. Plants need just the right amount of light. While some like full sun, others prefer partial shade or full shade.

Your plants will also need water. Find a place where you can water your plant with a watering can. Make sure you are close to a sink or faucet, so you don't have to carry the water too far.

Once you have a good sunny spot, you can look for a container. This part is fun. You can use anything that holds dirt. You can use clay or plastic pots. You can also use recycled tin cans and plastic bottles.

Old rain boots make cute containers. Put holes in the bottom for drainage. Set them on your front step to show people a gardener lives there.

Look around your house for interesting containers. You can plant flowers in old shoes, or grow tomatoes in a basket lined with plastic. You can build wooden boxes, or you can plant a garden in a bucket. Just make sure your family approves of your container

before you plant. You don't want to make your sister mad by using her good tennis shoes.

Any container you choose will need to have a hole in the bottom. This will help the plant's roots. Sometimes gardeners can overwater, which can kill their plants. If you put a hole in the container, the extra water will drain out. Then the plant will stay healthy.

Hanging pots and baskets are easy to care for. Excess water can easily drain right out of the bottom.

Water catchers, or plant saucers, can save your floors from water stains and muddy messes. This will keep your parents happy, too.

If your container does not have a hole, ask an adult to cut one for you. He or she may have to use a drill or nail. Make the hole a half inch wide.

You will also need to put a water catcher under your container. If you overwater your plants, the water will drain into the water catcher. Look for plastic trays or plates that will fit under your containers. You can use old plastic lids or butter tubs, or you can buy plant saucers at a garden store.

Chapter
Chapter 2

Tools and Supplies

You will need special tools and supplies to build your container garden. You can find them at garden stores, or you can save money and buy used tools at garage sales. Make sure the tools are in good shape. Metal tools last longer than plastic tools, but you must dry them after use, so they will not rust.

Some gardeners like to dig in the dirt with their bare hands. They like the feel of mud and soil. Other gardeners like to keep their fingernails clean. Both types of gardeners need gloves to protect their hands. Some plants have stickers or thorns that can poke and scratch. Containers can break and cut you. Gloves can save you from painful scrapes and sores.

A container gardener needs a **trowel** (TROW-ul). A trowel is a small shovel with a short handle that fits nicely in your hand. You can use it to move soil and dig holes for your plants.

You should also buy a watering can. Plastic watering cans work best for kids because they are lightweight. Make sure your watering can comes with a **sprinkler head**. This is a flat, round piece of plastic that fits onto the end of the spout. Holes in it let water sprinkle gently onto your

plants. Be careful when watering your container garden. If you pour the water out fast and hard, it can break stems and leaves.

Scissors are another handy tool. You can use them to **prune** your plants when they get too big. You can cut off dead leaves and dried stems.

Every garden needs labels to help you remember plant names and the date you planted seeds. You can make labels from craft sticks or cut them from cardboard.

Another supply you will need is soil. Soil holds food and water for the plants. The roots of a plant take in the food and water and send it to the leaves. Do not dig soil from the ground. Instead, use **potting soil**. This specially mixed soil is sold in bags at gardening stores. It contains nutrients that will feed your container plants. Potting soil is clean. It does not have **pollutants**, which are chemicals that can harm plants.

You will need a supply of **mulch**. Mulch is tiny pieces of wood and leaves. A layer of mulch will help your container garden hold water so that it does not dry out too fast. Too much water can kill plants. Letting the roots dry out will harm plants, too.

Garden Tip

Talk to the people who work at garden centers. They know about plants. They can also give you information about tools and supplies.

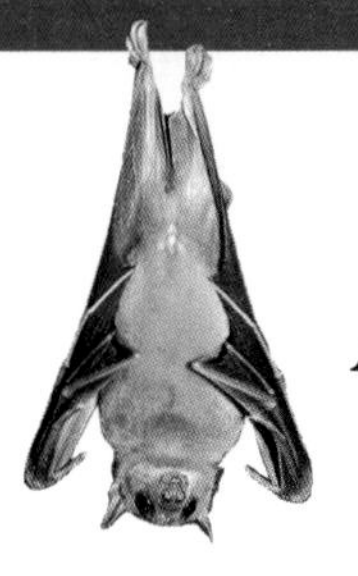

A fruit bat

Plants that live in containers sometimes need extra food called **fertilizer** (FUR-tuh-ly-zer). **Organic** fertilizer is best. *Organic* means it is natural, and not made of chemicals. Some natural fertilizers are bat and bird **guano**. (*Guano* is another word for poop.) Some fertilizers are made from seaweed or kale. Other fertilizers are made from bones or dried fish. It is important to wear gloves and then wash your hands after you use any type of fertilizer.

Keep your supplies and tools neat and tidy. You can make a tool kit from a plastic storage box. Use a permanent marker to write a list of your tools and supplies. You can write on the box or on a piece of paper that you tape to the box. Ask your family to help you find a good place to store your tool kit.

Chapter
Chapter
3

Choosing Your Plants

Once you have your tools and supplies, it is time to choose some plants for your container garden. It is important to remember that plants are living things. They eat, breathe, and grow. You need to have the right conditions to help your plants thrive.

Some plants, called annuals, grow for one season. Others are biennial (by-EH-nee-ul), which means they grow one season, flower the next season, then die. Perennials (PER-eh-nee-uls) will come back year after year. Some perennials die back in winter, then return each spring. Other perennials grow all year long for several years.

Almost all plants like spring and summer weather. There is plenty of sunshine and the air is warm. When it gets cold and the temperature drops below freezing, most plants will die. If your container garden is outside, you can move it inside. Or you can leave it outside and let your garden go **dormant**. *Dormant* means the plants are no longer growing. You can plant new seedlings in the spring.

If your plants are inside, keep them warm. When it is cold, keep them away from windows, or put a piece of cardboard in the window at

night to protect the plants from drafts. Take out the cardboard each morning to let in the sunlight.

You will need to decide what kind of plants you want to grow. You can grow fruits, vegetables, **herbs**, or flowers. These are all good plants for container gardens.

Garden Tip

Don't be afraid to try new seeds and plants. Good gardeners like to experiment. You can learn from mistakes as well as from successes.

Tomatoes grow well in containers. Make sure you put a stake or tomato cage in the pot. This will help the plants stand up.

Gardeners love cyclamen plants. These tropical houseplants bloom in the winter and brighten up the world with their flowers.

Peppers make colorful container plants. You can use them in a salad.

It is fun to grow vegetables. You can eat what you grow. Tomatoes, peppers, and lettuce are all plants that will grow well in containers. If you grow these plants, you can make your own salad. Vegetables grow best outdoors.

Some vegetables with vines—such as cucumbers, yellow squash, and zucchini—will grow in containers. You must have enough space for the vines to spread out. If you have lots of space, you can grow small pumpkins.

It is hard to grow **root crops** in containers. Root crops are plants that have roots people can eat, such as carrots, radishes, and turnips. If you like these vegetables, try **dwarf** plants, which are smaller. The vegetables will be small, but the dwarf plants will grow better in a container.

Strawberries grow well in containers. It takes two years for most strawberry plants to grow fruit, but they are worth the wait. You can also grow blueberries, raspberries, and even dwarf apple and cherry trees in containers. For trees you will need a very large container—about 24 inches high and 18 inches across.

Herbs are plants that are used to flavor food. There are many herbs that will grow in containers. Oregano is used in Italian food—it tastes good with pasta and on pizza. Rosemary and sage are used to

Herbs such as rosemary are easy to grow. Their leaves have a delightful scent that can be released just by touching the plant.

Coleus are shade-loving plants with brightly colored leaves. You don't have to have flowers to make an attractive container garden.

flavor chicken and turkey. Dill is used to flavor pickles. Lavender and mint are used to make teas. Basil and thyme are also popular cooking herbs. You can grow all of these plants in a container.

You may want to grow flowers to make your home look pretty. There are lots of flowers you can use. Marigolds and zinnias can be grown from seed. The seeds can be planted in small containers and kept inside until the weather warms up. Once the seedlings have their second set of leaves, you can **transplant** them to bigger containers, where they will have more room to grow.

Petunias grow quickly. By early summer, they fill their containers with flowers that will last until late fall.

Other plants, such as geraniums and petunias, grow best when you buy them as seedlings. You can also try begonias, lantana, or snapdragons. All of these plants come in many colors and grow well in containers.

Bulbs are another choice for container gardens. You can plant summer-growing bulbs in the spring, and they will bloom all summer. Take them inside during cold weather to keep them from freezing.

Tulip bulbs are planted outside in the fall. They need to be out in the cold winter weather to bloom in the spring.

Caladiums are plants with huge colorful leaves. Gardeners often call them elephant ears because they look so similar to the giant animal's ears.

Some bulbs that grow well in containers are cannas, calla lilies, and gladiolas.

Elephant ears are fun to grow from bulbs. They do not flower, but they grow leaves as big as an elephant's ear. They get so big, you can sit under them.

Chapter 4

Ready to Grow

Once you have learned about plants, you are ready for the fun part—digging in the dirt. Building your container garden is easy when you have all your supplies and tools. The next step is to get your container ready.

Wash your container to make sure it is clean. Remember you need to have a hole a half-inch wide in the bottom. Line the bottom of your container with a few rocks or pebbles to keep the hole clear of soil. Next, add a layer of wood mulch. For a small container, you will need an inch or two of mulch. If you have a big container, you will need three or four inches. Fill the rest of the container with potting soil. Then add plants.

Use a variety of plants to make your container garden interesting. Look for plants with different colored flowers, or pick plants with different shaped leaves. You might like a pink and purple garden, or maybe a rainbow garden. Be creative and use your imagination.

Choose flowers that will grow well together. Be sure to plant sun-loving flowers with other plants that like light. Do not mix sun plants and shade plants. Be sure they need about the same

You can make a simple container garden using just one type of plant. Choose a bright pot to go with whatever you are planting, then follow these easy steps:

1. *Gather your supplies: plants, soil, mulch, rocks, small shovel or spoon.*
2. *Make sure your container is clean.*
3. *Line the bottom of the container with rocks.*
4. *Add a layer of mulch.*
5. *Fill the rest of the container with potting soil.*
6. *Add your plant, press it into the soil, and water it.*
7. *Then show off your beautiful container garden.*

amount of water as well. Plants that like wet soil cannot grow in dry dirt.

For example, you can plant petunias, marigolds, and daisies in the same container because they all

like bright sun. Impatiens and coleus will grow well together because they like shade. Begonias can grow in either sun or shade. They can be planted with violets or vinca plants. Be sure to read the plant labels or seed packets to find out about each plant's sun and water needs.

You can also create container gardens that have a theme. If you like Mexican food, you can plant a **salsa** garden. Plant tomatoes in the center of this garden. (Cherry tomatoes grow very well in containers.) Add some pepper plants. You can use jalapeño peppers, which are very hot and spicy, or banana peppers, which are mild and sweet. On the outside edge of the container, plant some cilantro, an herb that is used in making salsa. All of these plants like sunshine. When the peppers and tomatoes are ripe, you can pick them. Mix them with cilantro to make your own salsa.

Garden Tip

Garden catalogs are free and they give lots of information about plants. You can order garden catalogs online. Your library will also have books about plants.

Another fun theme is a soup garden. You can pick the vegetables and make soup. Put a long stick in the middle of your pot, and put bean plants by the stick. The bean vines will grow up the stick.

Next plant some cherry tomatoes. At the edge of the pot, plant some basil, which is an herb used to flavor soups. All of these plants like lots of sun.

You can make a shade garden with plants that don't need much light. Plant a hosta in the middle of your pot. Most hostas have large leaves. They do not have big flowers, but they are a pretty plant. Next to the hosta, plant some impatiens. These plants come in many colors and flower from spring until fall. You can plant several colors together, such as white, pink, and red.

You may want to plant a surprise garden. Look around the garden store. Find vegetables you have never eaten and plant those vegetable plants. When they are ripe, you can cook them with your family. It will be a surprise for your taste buds. You could plant squash, eggplant, or zucchini. You could try bell peppers, okra, or Brussels sprouts. All of these plants like the sun.

Hosta

You can make any kind of garden you want. Just remember to read seed packets or the labels on your plants. Only put plants together if they like the same kind of light. Make sure they need the same amount of water. If you follow these steps, you will be on your way to having a beautiful garden.

Chapter
Chapter
5

Keeping Them Growing

Once you have planted your container garden, it is important to keep it growing. You need to make sure your garden has enough food, water, and sunlight. You must also watch for insects and weeds that can harm your plants.

Container gardens dry out faster than gardens planted in the ground. Check the soil in your container. It should be moist to the touch. If the soil is dry and pulling away from the edge of the pot, your garden needs water. Another sign that plants need water is when they **wilt**. When a plant wilts, its leaves droop and look saggy. Wilting shows the plant does not have enough water in its stems and leaves to stand up straight.

Remember to keep track of the amount of sunlight your garden is getting. If the leaves of your plants look yellow instead of green, they may need more light. The good thing about a container garden is that you can move your plants to give them more or less light. It's pretty hard to move a garden planted in the ground.

Plants living in containers need more food than plants in the ground. Plants in the ground get **nutrients** from leaves that fall on the ground and from worms working the soil. Plants in pots

Tulips bloom early in the spring before most weeds have a chance to grow. Tulips are low maintenance.

can't get nutrients from those places, so you must help them by adding fertilizer. The instructions for how to use the fertilizer are on the bag. Make sure you have an adult help you with fertilizer, wear gloves, and wash your hands after using it.

Weeds are any plants that you don't want to grow in your garden. Weeds take food from the flowers or vegetables you are trying to grow. The best way to get rid of weeds is to pull them out. Grab the weed at the spot where the leaves meet the soil, then gently pull out the roots as well as the leaves and stems. Throw the weed away.

Insects can be another problem for your garden.

Check your plants frequently to see if they need water. Your plants will need more water in warm weather and less in cool weather. Always touch the soil first to see if it is dry.

Take care of your plants by removing dead leaves and flowers. Pull any weeds that have sprouted in your pot.

Although some people find them creepy looking, praying mantises are helpful to the garden. They eat insects that will damage your plants.

Some insects are good for plants. For example, bees help plants grow and make seeds. Other insects can damage plants by eating them. Check your plants often to see if insects are harming them. If you see insects on your plants, you can pick them off. You may want to use gloves when you do this.

If you are a good gardener, your plants may grow so well that they get too big for their pots. If this happens, you will need to transplant your garden. Vegetable plants can stay in the same pot for the whole season, but you may need to transplant flowers and herbs.

When you transplant, you will need extra soil and mulch. Make sure you loosen the roots of your

Anything can become a container. This old milk can has been turned into a large pot for flowers. It uses the typical strawberry container shape of small holes placed around the sides.

plant before you put them in the new container. The larger pot will give the roots room to grow. Your flowers will look bigger and better than before.

During cold weather, you may decide to try to bring some of your plants inside. Herbs grow well inside if they have a sunny window.

Garden Tip

For many more ideas of what you can add to make your garden extra special, check out Garden Crafts for Kids: 50 Great Reasons to Get Your Hands Dirty, *by Diane Rhoades.*

Being a gardener is fun. You can see the results of your work when your plants are big and healthy. As a gardener, you will learn about nature and help make the world a beautiful place.

You can mix containers of flowers to decorate windowsills or patios.

No matter what type of plants you want to grow, you can add color to your garden by decorating the containers. Use waterproof paint to decorate pots, baskets, or coffee cans.

Some flowers, like geraniums, can live indoors, but vegetable plants will not grow well inside.

Many container gardeners simply leave their plants outside all winter. The plants will freeze and die, but the gardeners put new plants out every spring. Gardeners like looking at catalogs of plants and flowers during the winter. They plan what they will plant when it gets warm. That way they can enjoy working with their gardens all year long.

If you plant a container garden, you may have so much fun that you decide to become a lifelong gardener. Then you can have a lifetime full of flowers, vegetables, and messing around in the mud.

Craft

Make Your Own Dried Flowers and Garden Tools

You can have fun making tools for your garden, and drying the flowers you grow.

Dried Flowers

Collecting and pressing flowers is a way to keep a part of your garden forever. You can use dried flowers to make pictures and gifts for your family. You will need an old phone book, a pair of scissors, tweezers, craft glue, craft paper, and a storage box.

When your flowers are blooming, cut a few of the blossoms to dry them. Some flowers that work well are pansies, violets, coreopsis, and roses. Place the cut flowers on separate pages of the phone book. Once you have put all your flowers in the book, close it tight and place it in a warm, dry place for two weeks. This will allow the flowers to completely dry.

When your flowers are dry, use tweezers to gently place them in the bottom of a cardboard storage box. If you plan to dry lots of flowers, you can make paper folders for each kind of flower. Always store your flowers by laying them flat and keeping them in a dry place.

You can use your dried flowers to make pictures or note cards for you friends. Arrange the flowers on craft paper. After you have the flowers where you want them, lift each one and put a few dots of glue under it. Press the flowers down with your fingers. Let the glue dry. Then write a note to your friends. They will love the real flower picture.

Rain Gauge

A rain gauge is a tool that measures the amount of water that falls when it rains. You can make your own rain gauge with a few simple supplies: a permanent marker, a ruler, and a glass jar with straight sides.

Stand the ruler up against the jar. Use the marker to make lines on the jar at quarter-inch, half-inch, three-quarter-inch, and one-inch spaces. Continue marking the jar until you reach the top. Let the marks on the jar dry.

When the jar is dry, set it outside near your garden. Wait until it rains. After the rain ends, go out and check your rain gauge. Look at the line closest to the top of the water. This tells you how much rain fell on your garden. You can listen to the weather report and check to see if your rain gauge measures the same as the scientists' gauges.

Wind Sock

You can also make a **wind sock**, a tool that shows the direction the wind is blowing. It can also be used to decorate your garden. You will need **adult help** to make this project. You will need a glue gun, a two-foot square of nylon cloth, scissors, chenille stems, four yards of ribbon, a dowel rod, and two feet of string.

Fold the cloth in half and glue the open edge to make a sleeve. Let it dry. Then twist together the chenille stems to make a ring five inches wide. Place the ring at one end of the sleeve. Fold the edge of the nylon over the chenille stems and glue it down. This makes the opening of the wind sock.

Cut the ribbon into two-foot strips. Glue the strips to the end of the windsock that is opposite the chenille stems. To fly the wind sock, make a notch in one end of the dowel rod. Make a slipknot in the middle of the string. Cut tiny holes on each side of the top of the wind sock. Push one end of the string through each hole and tie it. Put the end of the string in the notch on the dowel rod. Place the other end of the dowel rod into the soil in one of your pots. Watch your wind sock fly!

Further Reading

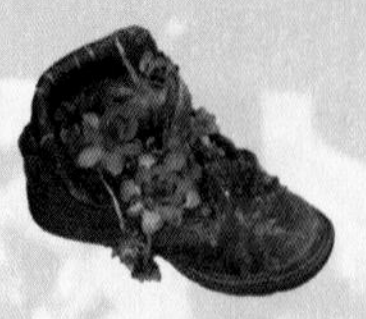

Books

Bull, Jane. *The Gardening Book.* New York: DK Publishing, 2003.

Krezel, Cindy. *Kids' Container Gardening.* Batavia, Illinois: Ball Publishing, 2005.

Lovejoy, Sharon. *Roots, Shoots, Buckets & Boots.* New York: Workman Publishing, 1999.

Matthews, Clare. *How Does Your Garden Grow? Great Gardening for Green-Fingered Kids.* London: Hamlyn Publishing, 2005.

Morris, Karyn. *The Kids Can Press Jumbo Book of Gardening.* Toronto, Ontario: Kids Can Press, 2000.

Spohn, Rebecca. *Ready, Set, Grow! A Kid's Guide to Gardening.* Tucson, Arizona: Good Year Books, 2007.

Works Consulted

Ball, Liz. *Step-By-Step Garden Basics.* Des Moines, Iowa: Better Homes and Gardens Books, 2000.

Barash, Cathy Wilkinson. *Choosing Plant Combinations.* Des Moines, Iowa: Better Homes and Gardens Books, 1999.

Brown, Kathleen. *Seasonal Container Gardening.* London: Penguin Publishing, 1991.

Le Bailly, Pamela. *Pressed Flowers.* Jersey City, New Jersey: David Porteous Editions, 1999.

Ouellet, Kerstin P. *Contain Yourself.* Batavia, Illinois: Ball Publishing, 2003.

Ryrie, Charlie, and Cindy Engel. *The Gaia Book of Organic Gardening.* London: Gaia Books Ltd., 2005.

Schenk, George. *Gardening on Pavement, Tables, and Hard Surfaces.* Portland, Oregon: Timber Press, 2003.

Yang, Linda. *The City Gardener's Handbook.* North Adams, Massachusetts: Storey Publishing, 2002.

On the Internet

Container Gardening Guru
http://www.containergardeningguru.com/

Kiddie Gardening: "Types of Gardening Containers"
http://www.kiddiegardens.com/gardening_containers.html

Kids Gardening: "Gardening in Containers"
http://www.kidsgardening.com/growingideas/projects/feb03/pg1.html

USDA Hardiness Zone Maps
http://www.growit.com/zones/

"Windowsill Garden," Family Fun Magazine
http://jas.familyfun.go.com/arts-and-crafts?page=CraftDisplay&craftid=11511

Photo Credits: Cover, pp. 30–31—Catherine Opladen; pp. 1, 2, 3, 6, 7, 12, 28, 38, 44–48 (background)—Barbara Marvis; pp. 8, 13, 18, 34, 39, 41—JupiterImages; p. 11–Tamra Orr; p. 23—Emely/Getty Images; p. 27—Janet DiGiacomo; p. 37—Amie Jane Leavitt; pp. 44, 45—Stephanie Bearce. All other photos—Creative Commons. Every effort has been made to locate all copyright holders of material used in this book. If any errors or omissions have occurred, corrections will be made in future editions of this book.

Glossary

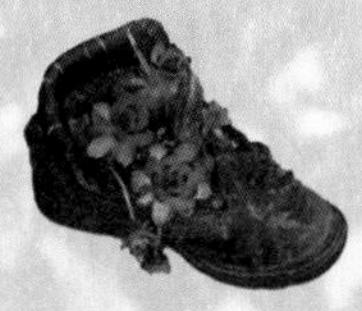

archaeologist (ar-kee-AH-loh-jist)—A person who studies people who lived in the past by looking at ancient objects.

bulb—A short underground stem surrounded by small leaves that holds stored food for the plant.

container garden (kun-TAY-ner GAR-den)—Small groups of plants that are grown in a pot, tub, or wooden box.

dormant (DOR-ment)—At a stage in a plant's life when growth slows or stops.

dwarf (DWORF) **plants**—Plants that are smaller than standard size.

fertilizer (FUR-tuh-ly-zer)—A food that is added to soil to help plants grow.

guano (GWAH-noh)—Droppings of birds or bats.

hardiness (HAR-dee-ness) **zone**—One of the areas of different climates that may or may not be suitable for certain plants.

herbs (URBS)—Plants that are used to flavor foods.

mulch (MULCH)—A layer of shredded wood and leaves that protects plants.

nutrients (NOO-tree-unts)—Food for plants or animals.

organic (or-GAN-ik)—relating to or coming from nature.

pollutants (puh-LOO-tants)—The chemicals that damage soil, plants, and animals.

portable (POR-tuh-bul)—Easy to move from one place to another.

potting soil (POT-ing SOYL)—Dirt that is specially mixed with nutrients and used for growing plants.

prune (PROON)—To cut or trim plants.

root crops—Plants grown for the food contained in their roots.

salsa (SOL-sah)—A spicy sauce.

seedlings—Young plants.

soil (SOYL)—Dirt or ground that holds food for plants.

sprinkler (SPRINK-lur) **head**—A flat round piece of plastic with holes that can be attached to the end of a watering can.

transplant (TRANS-plant)—To move a plant from a small container to a larger container.

trowel (TROW-ul)—A small shovel with a short handle that is used to dig holes for plants.

wilt—To droop from lack of water.

wind sock—A tool used to tell which way the wind is blowing.

Index